**'Are you ready? Are you ready?
Are you Red, Red, ready?'**

Words and Photos By Dawn Marlow

I0419283

Copyright © 2017 by Dawn Marlow. 731292

Library of Congress Control Number: 2016902300

ISBN: Softcover   978-1-5144-4582-2
        Hardcover   978-1-5144-4584-6
        EBook   978-1-5144-4583-9

All rights reserved. No part of this book may
be reproduced or transmitted in any form or by
any means, electronic or mechanical, including
photocopying, recording, or by any information storage
and retrieval system, without permission in writing from
the copyright owner.

Red was rescued by the Author from an Animal
Welfare Centre. The photographs are of Queenscliff,
Victoria, Australia.

Print information available on the last page

Rev. date: 07/26/2017

To order additional copies of this book, contact:
Xlibris
1-800-455-039
www.xlibris.com.au
Orders@Xlibris.com.au

'Hi, my name is Sir Redmond. You may call me Red. I'm having a bit of a stretch before I go for my walk. Are you ready? Are you ready? Are you Red, Red, ready?'

What a beautiful, sunny day! The flowers are out and I can't resist smelling them.
Do you like smelling flowers?

I love smelling fresh grass too. There are parks, beaches and a bay where I live. I'm heading for the steps that lead to the beach.

Past the old lighthouse, down these steep steps, and I'm nearly there! Do you know what a lighthouse does?

4

These steps are longer than I thought!
Ahh, here I am at one of my favourite spots.
Where is your favourite place?

Before we start exploring, there is
something I have to do. Now that's better!
Sometimes I really need to scratch my back.
Have you ever had an itchy back?

Oh, and just one more thing, if you don't mind? I do need a little privacy though, but then I'll be right with you. Thankyou.

There are some people on the beach. And rocks and cliffs to explore. I have to be very careful as the rocks can be slippery. Do you like to climb?

I wonder why there is so much seaweed today? What do you think? Let's head for the fishing pier now.

Excuse me Sir, 'How's the fishing?' He seems to be concentrating on putting his bait on the hook.

I wonder if you catch more fish from a pier or a boat?

I have to be careful I don't get too near to the edge. Are you careful near water?
Hang on! I think I just saw a stingray! Have you ever seen a stingray?

Look how low the tide is! There isn't any sand here, just rocks and mud. The seagulls like it. I like it too.

The old yacht club looks like a fun place to explore.
What's over this log?
Only dust under here...

The wind has blown up and I feel like running.

I'm running very fast...

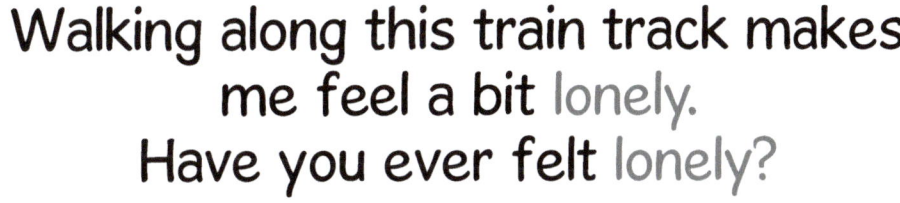

Walking along this train track makes me feel a bit lonely.
Have you ever felt lonely?

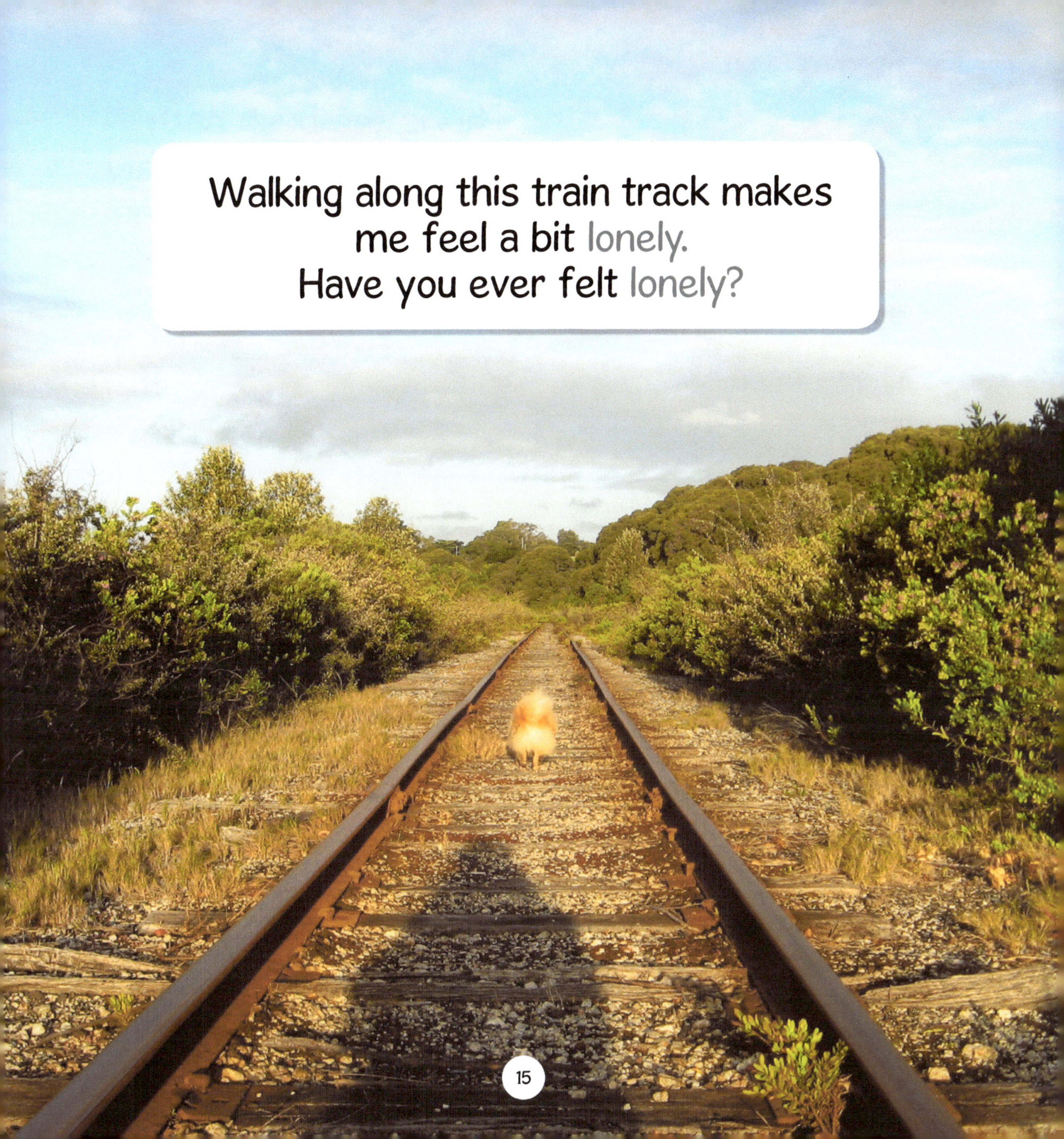

This is the bush path which winds past the new lighthouse. Can you see any differences between the old lighthouse and this one?

I'm staying on the boardwalk!
This grass is spiky!

I love trees! Do you?

Hey, there's my friend Patch. He's a fast runner too!

Up the garden path...
a quick stop for a 'selfie'...

I'm Home!

20

Walking is great fun...sorry, can't keep my eyes open...zzzzzzz

www.ingramcontent.com/pod-product-compliance
Lightning Source LLC
Chambersburg PA
CBHW060827290526
45792CB00005BB/1835